WALID AKKAD

BESTIAIRE

Graphic Creation
Habib Charaf
Octopus Design Flow

Photographs
Jeremy Zenou
Atelier MAI 98

Silvana Editoriale

Direction
Dario Cimorelli

Art Director
Giacomo Merli

Editorial Coordinator
Sergio Di Stefano, Giulia Mercanti

Copy Editing
Laura Maggioni

Production Coordinator
Antonio Micelli

Photo Editor
Silvia Sala

Press Office
Alessandra Olivari, press@silvanaeditoriale.it

All reproduction and translation rights
reserved for all countries
© 2022 Silvana Editoriale S.p.A.,
Cinisello Balsamo, Milano
© Walid Akkad

Under copyright and civil law this volume
cannot be reproduced, wholly or in part,
in any form, original or derived, or by any
means: print, electronic, digital, mechanical,
including photocopy, microfilm, film or any
other medium, without permission in writing
from the publisher.

Silvana Editoriale S.p.A.
via dei Lavoratori, 78
20092 Cinisello Balsamo, Milano
tel. 02 453 951 01
www.silvanaeditoriale.it

Reproductions, printing
and binding in Italy

Printed October 2022

WALID AKKAD

BESTIAIRE

Text & preface
Michael Jakob

SilvanaEditoriale

Preface

Walid Akkad has imagined a spectacular bestiary made up of twenty-one animals, both small and large. Through his artistic medium of creative jewellery, Akkad has developed a system centred around a minimalist vision. His rings, the bull for example, don't just represent an animal through illustration but by using metonymy. In the case of the bull, the animal's horns alone are enough for us to recognize it. "Take the bull by the horns" immediately comes to mind. Or its force, its vitality. Danger and fascination. Bullfights too, and the minotaur. Europa, abducted by the bull. The constellation of Taurus.

And so, a tiny, subtle sign added to a ring is enough to open up a whole universe. By being iconic and non-verbal, this sign, characteristic of each individual ring, is open to an infinite number of interpretations. The sign Taurus can mean something to both a woman or a man, a European or an inhabitant of another continent, to a lover of mythology or horoscopes, to people both young and old. The essence of these tiny works of art is precisely their capacity to impose nothing in particular, to be nothing more than an invitation on a delectable voyage to the depths of our own imagination.

Moreover, human beings have undoubtedly the closest relationship with the animal kingdom. We love, hunt, breed, exhibit, collect, use animals, sometimes believing they have a soul, sometimes seeing them as our best friends, or (relatively recently) as living beings worthy of our respect.

One of the most important characteristics of our vision of animals is that when we look at them, we are in fact, looking at ourselves. From the fables of Aesop and La Fontaine, not forgetting those in fairy tales, even in comic strips, manga and animation films, animals are always by our side. This common ground, where human and animal qualities are superimposed, holds an essential place in our imaginations. Just one word is enough to conjure up a whole universe in our minds, taking on a specific appearance with just one particular animal.

The term "wolf", for example, conjures up a whole sphere which, within a cultural system, assigns certain positive or negative qualities to this animal whether it's the famous wolf from Dante's Comedy, the one in *Little Red Riding Hood*, or even a real wolf who attacks other animals.

In the vast ocean of our imagination filled with all kinds of concepts, the words (and forms) used to describe animals have a different function. Using the term "cat" or "dog", saying "snake" or "mouse" now has certain implications, notably physiological. There are those who, on just hearing the word "mouse", start to shake with fear, whilst others, on reading the word "snake", can already feel the increasing closeness of the slithering creature. However, these same people appear to have no problems with domains of verbal or iconic representation where the mouse is a cute little friend, snakes are the symbol of medicine, owls the sign of intelligence, bulls the image of strength, and so on.

We might quite rightly talk about anthropomorphism here, whilst forgetting nonetheless that the phenomenon in question is, in itself, a complex cultural construction. In the mythical stages of humanity there were phases where animal forms and humans forms mixed together.

We could make reference to ancient Egypt where the gods had the bodies of a human with an animal's head, and that had been the case since early ancient history around 2700 years BC., so a very long time before the Greeks! In the "zoology" of the Greeks, there was an attempt to obathe place of one animal or another in the system of nature (why did God create the scorpion? or flies?), all of this becoming sedimented in our memories along with the traces of domestication. In addition, doesn't the animal kingdom appear completely domesticated today? A catalogue for which we humans are now responsible?

Walid Akkad's astonishing bestiary shows in any case that animals can still surprise us in the age of the Anthropocene.

Michael Jakob

The Shellfish

The Caterpillar

The Hedgehog

The Hen

The Ladybug

The Mouse

The Dolphin

The Snake

The Butterfly

The Crocodile

The Bird

The Rabbit

The Giraffe

The Horse

The Ram

The Elk

The Elephant

The Bull

The Owl

The Night Butterfly

The Octopus

The plural form of the word "shellfish" refers to the large number of sea molluscs who live in shells. This rather vague scientific category includes cockles, mussels, oysters, scallops, razor clams, limpets, to name but a few of the best-known ones. These aquatic animals can be univalve or bivalve and are made up of a hard bio-mineral exterior containing a soft body.

Due to the variety of shapes, colours and textures, these shellfish have long been used as elements for making jewellery and as bargaining chips, becoming the favourite object of collectors during the Renaissance. Nautilus, in particular, were the pride and glory of cabinets of curiosities, and later became one of the inspirations for the exuberant jewellery created in the seventeenth and eighteenth centuries. Shells were also the main material used for ancient cameos, a tradition brought back to life in ewers crafted from coloured or engraved mother-of-pearl.

Shellfish are so widely used that we sometimes forget the essential role they play in the field of culture, one which goes far beyond their culinary or decorative use. For example, the famous scallop or "Saint Jacques" (*Pecten maximus*) which has become the symbol of the pilgrimage to Galicia, where the apostle Saint James died.

Bringing back a shell became the tangible proof of the completed journey, whilst the richest pilgrims bought a gold or silver shell at the Plaza de las Platerías. The shell, sometimes placed on the pilgrim's coat, testified to the almost mystical encounter with the sea and the Virgin Mary who, by giving birth to Christ, created a "pearl" out of the symbiosis of the Earth and the Heavens.

In a more prosaic but nonetheless just as significant sense, fossilised shells were at the centre of a passionate scientific and philosophical debate. By analysing spiral-shaped shells and noting that a small number of them turned in the wrong direction, to the left, this anomaly acted as a catalyst for teleological thought.

Were both nature and the universe – with the shell as its reflection – going in a certain direction? Mathematics and beauty also crossed paths when the history of the earth, founded on the existence of fossilised molluscs found in high mountains, emerged, thus transgressively contributing to the deconstruction of the Great Flood myth.

And lastly, let's not forget, the invention of the term "baroque". It came into the vocabulary of jewellery makers in the sixteenth century, taken from the Portuguese word *barroco*, used to define pearls which were not perfectly round. This critical concept established itself and signified so much more than simply a period of European art.

THE SHELLFISH

Becoming the favorite object of collectors during the Renaissance.

*I*n chapter IV of Lewis Carroll's book, Alice, lost in Wonderland, has a determining encounter. It was in fact the caterpillar who enabled her to understand for the first time the problems of scale she experiences throughout her adventures and the possibility of changing size.

The episode in questions starts like this: "She stretched herself up on tiptoe, and peeped over the edge of the mushroom, and her eyes immediately met those of a large caterpillar, that was sitting on the top with its arms folded, quietly smoking a long hookah, and taking not the smallest notice of her or of anything else." The meeting between Alice and the blue caterpillar began with the famous question: "Who Are You?", to which the young girl could not answer and so the conversation continued in dribs and drabs as the caterpillar was not very talkative and rather stubborn.

The well-known illustration by John Tenniel combines the "facial" features of the personified caterpillar with the phallic "body" of a larva sitting on top of a large mushroom cap. Together with the arabesque shaped hookah, the mushroom led to the idea that Carroll's fairyland world had been influenced by drugs.

The caterpillar represents one of four evolving phases: it all starts with the egg, often laid by the moth on tree trunks (but sometimes even on the ground or on leaves), then comes the caterpillar followed by the chrysalis and the butterfly. The passage to caterpillar (from the Latin *canicula*, meaning little dog) is the stage when the caterpillar eats excessively and grows. During this same period, the caterpillar astonishingly sheds its skin several times. But it doesn't just shed its skin, it sloughs its entire envelope, its skull, jawbones (essential because all it does is eat), eyes, barbels, antenna…

Caterpillars spin from birth, or better, secrete a liquid that surrounds them. Once dried in the air, it becomes the cocoon, protecting them throughout pupation. The most famous cocoon being of course the silkworm's. Caterpillars spend the winter without eating or moving. When the cold closes in, it covers itself in a light cocoon, lined inside with silk. All caterpillar bodies are divided up into twelve rings; most of them have a singular, large, coloured stripe running down the length of their backs.

The magnificent play of colours makes these larvae a biological gem with a mimetic function that allows them to blend into their host environment. Alice's blue caterpillar recalls the blue and black of a caterpillar species which is hardly ever attacked by its numerous enemies because of its strange colour. This chromatism is due to a plant eaten by caterpillars; our little shapeshifter is in fact protected by a toxic plant.

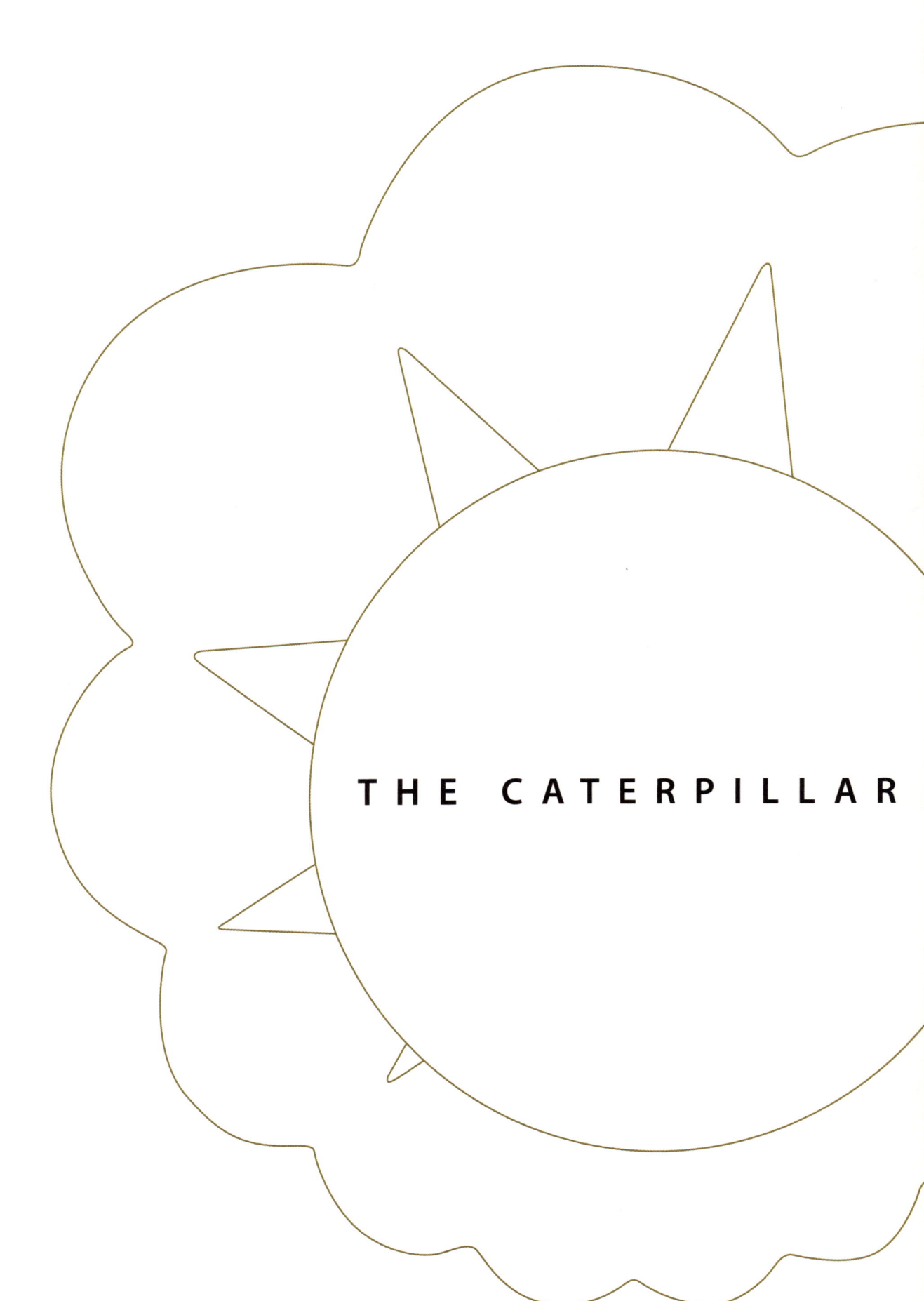

*When the cold closes in, it covers itself in a light cocoon,
lined inside with silk.*

For William Shakespeare, the word "hedgehog" was an insult. In *Alice in Wonderland*, the Queen of Cards plays cricket with hedgehogs. In the Middle Ages, the English considered hedgehogs to be a witch's ally and chased them out. Mongolian legend tells how three animals – a wolf, a fox, and a hedgehog – were fighting over some fruit, and it was the hedgehog who beat the other two. However, the Mongolians didn't like this animal, because finding one in your home was a bad omen.

One of Grimm's fairy tales on the other hand, recounts how a hedgehog managed to beat a rabbit in a race, the moral of the story being to never underestimate your adversaries. In the children's novel *Good Little Girls*, the Comtesse de Ségur tells the story of a noble family in the nineteenth century, who were deeply pained when the gamekeeper Nicaire sacrifices four hedgehogs. The latter defines the animals thrown into the garden pond as a "mean species" and adds: "They must be destroyed".

Fortunately, today the general trend is to try and save these animals who have been celebrated since the 1970s as one of the symbols of the ecosystem and the need to protect them. Hedgehogs were one of the very first mammals and they already attracted the attention of anonymous cave artists in ancient times. Active at night, these hunters are very useful in gardens, feeding off spiders, caterpillars, worms, ladybirds, but also wasps and snails.

Their most distinctive feature is undoubtedly their spikes and an adult hedgehog can have up to 7000 of them. They are in fact kinds of hollow hairs which act as a defence mechanism, because when a hedgehog is attacked it can roll up into a ball in a matter of seconds and remain in this position for almost twelve hours.

Like other animals, it is busy stocking up on its fat reserves until late autumn to get through the winter in hibernation. During this period, sometimes called the "little death", its usual body temperature (36° C) drops to 4° C.

In the Balkans, it is said that hedgehogs know the secret to finding the *raskovnik*, a rare medicinal herb with magical properties. Sometimes also called "hedgehog's grass", this plant, which according to legend looks like a four-leaved clover, can only be recognised by the initiated. The famous saying by the classical poet Archilochus: "a fox knows many things, but a hedgehog knows one big thing" was also taken up by the philosopher Isaiah Berlin. A defender of "hedgehogs", he believed that Plato, Lucretius, Dante, Pascal, Hegel, Nietzsche or even Proust were true hedgehog-thinkers.

THE HEDGEHOG

In Alice in Wonderland, *the Queen of Cards plays cricket with hedgehogs.*

Chickens, exotic animals originating in the Indies or Malaysia, were known in Egypt as early as the XVIII dynasty, at the time of Thutmose III (1479–1425 BC), who brought them back to his country during military campaigns in the Levant.

To discover the wonderful world of chickens, you just have to visit a poultry fair. The contestants in this kind of event are prepared a long time in advance because a show chicken must be at the height of its form, have magnificent feathers reflecting its good health and ideal weight. To this end, the chickens follow a special diet and are perfectly trained.

Chicken fairs create high levels of stress among the little wannabe starlets, because the birds are cooped up in small cages and ogled at by admirers and judges. Just one hysterical or panicked chicken is enough to spoil the atmosphere of a show. So, these chickens must be trained for being shown to humans and the best way to do this is to handle them every day, so they get used to being touched and held. A few days before the show, the chicken must be washed and its feathers covered in natural oil, without forgetting to trim its beak and claws.

Known for their sociability, chickens have always been a part of popular imagination, with particularly virtuous red hens, black hens, hens transformed into princesses, or even the famous hen with the golden eggs. The latter, mentioned for the first time by Aesop, supposedly laid a gold egg, but its owner killed the hen hoping to find a great lump of gold in its belly. Added to the frustration of finding nothing of any value was the loss of the precious animal itself.

The thing that first attracts our attention with chickens (and cocks) is their crest. This dermal excrescence on their heads is the visible expression of the animal's hormonal health, but is also used, among other things, to regulate body temperature. There are chickens with a single, double, triple, curly, v-shaped crest, and some with no crest at all.

The bucolic image of the docile hen foraging for food (chickens are omnivorous) is deceiving. In reality, chickens live in an extremely polarised perimeter, with a leader who dominates over the others, a second-in-command, and so on until the end of the pecking order. The strongest chickens impose themselves in the restricted space of the chicken coop, by confronting each other, either on a symbolic level – by making specific sounds, puffing up their feathers suddenly, thanks to what they represent –, or during a real cock fight. Today, organised cock fights, forbidden in Europe since Victorian times, allow people in many Asian countries to exorcise pent-up human violence.

THE HEN

*There are chickens with a single, double, triple, curly,
V-shaped crest, and some without.*

Coccinellids, from the Greek *kokkinos*, meaning scarlet red, have a surprisingly varied symbolic meaning. In Sweden, if one of these little creatures lands on a young girl's hand, she will soon be wed. In Scotland, popular tradition recounts how unmarried girls let a coccinellid land on their hand and say: "Fly away east or fly away west, and show me where lives the one I like best."

In English they are called "ladybirds" or "ladybugs", clearly associating them with the female gender. In other languages they are known as "Mary's beetle", "Mary's bird", or even "Our Lady's bird". This tiny Coleoptera, measuring between 1 and 10 millimetres, brings together two traditions: one, pagan, taking weddings, love, reproduction, desire, in short, sexuality as life's driving force; the other, Christian one, reminds us of Mary's virginity, undoubtedly alluding to the abundance of red clothing worn by the mother of Christ in Western painting.

In truth, the characteristic red of the ladybird refers to an ambiguity invented by nature itself. The bright colours covering this "God's little creature", as it was once called in France, act indeed as a defence mechanism, just like the toxins it produces to protect itself from lizards and other hungry rivals.

However, these "insignificant" little creatures, spread over every continent and with over more than 6000 species, are far from innocent. They are in fact formidable predators, earning them a prime position in the biological struggle. Since the end of the nineteenth century, ladybirds have been used in farming: their destructive action is highly efficient against the aphids and acarids that infest plants, particularly in late spring. One of the most astonishing talents of coccinellids is their ability to adapt rapidly to unfavourable conditions. If needs be, they can change their food diet, occasionally becoming lovers of sugary liquids, fruits or pollen.

Today, the European ladybird or *septempunctata* – the one with seven black spots on its red back – is rivalled by its Asian cousin *Harmonia axyridis*, the "harlequin ladybird", particularly aggressive, prolific and voracious. The harlequin variety devours everything it finds, including caterpillars, cochineals, moths, pollinating caterpillars, insects and beneficial indigenous species and, when necessary, it even goes as far as eating its seven-spotted kinsman. Without even knowing it, we are in fact amidst the war of the ladybirds.

THE LADYBUG

*Fly away East or fly away West,
and show me where lives my beloved.*

"It all started with a mouse", Walt Disney loved to say. The mouse in question, Mickey, was invented to replace Oswald, the lucky rabbit who belonged to Universal Pictures. After having turned down a male frog and a cow, Disney found the dream character in a mouse who had quietly set up home at the foot of the desk where he worked in Kansas. Initially going by the name of Mortimer, he became Mickey Mouse and conquered the whole world from 1928 onwards.

Mice, associated with the domestic sphere, have always haunted our imagination. First sign of the Chinese zodiac, the mouse is a pioneer and a conqueror; considered to be charismatic and pragmatic, it symbolizes shrewdness and intelligence, but also sheer determination and an unrivalled capacity for work. Embodying prosperity and order, it can nevertheless also transform into a sign of death.

In a founding myth of the Hellenistic period, mice are affiliated with Apollo. Indeed, the inhabitants of Hamaxitos worshipped Apollon Smintheus – the Apollo of mice – by dedicating a temple to him, with a nest of sacred white mice under the altar next to the god's sacrificial tripod. These animals, the "sons of the earth", are said to have guided humans in their conquest of unknown lands. The power of mice is so great that even Ares or Athena couldn't withstand their attack.

During the Enlightenment, a strange philosophical treaty dating from 1742, written by a certain Johann Alexander Döderlein, presented a scholarly discussion which attempted to show how these harmful animals were nonetheless part of Creation. Because we live in the "best of possible worlds", it is the temerity, salubrity, divinatory capacity and humour of mice that we should take into account and not the damage they cause.

This humanisation of our little friends with the excellent sense of smell – they are also talented swimmers and good singers, even though the sounds they make are inaudible to us – also appears in a magnificent little work by John Constable, *Mouse with a Piece of Cheese* (1824). The extreme realism of the scene, rendered using thick, monochrome greys, captures the mouse when he is concentrating his utmost attention on the object of his desire: a piece of cheese.

Without this instinct, it runs the risks that Kafka expressed in a parable: "'Ah', says the mouse, 'the world is getting smaller every day. In the beginning, it was so big that I was frightened, I carried on running and I was happy to finally see the walls in the distance, to the left and right, but these long walls followed on so quickly one after the other that I was already in the last room, and there, in the corner, was the trap I was heading towards'. – 'You only have to change direction', said the cat, as he gobbled him up".

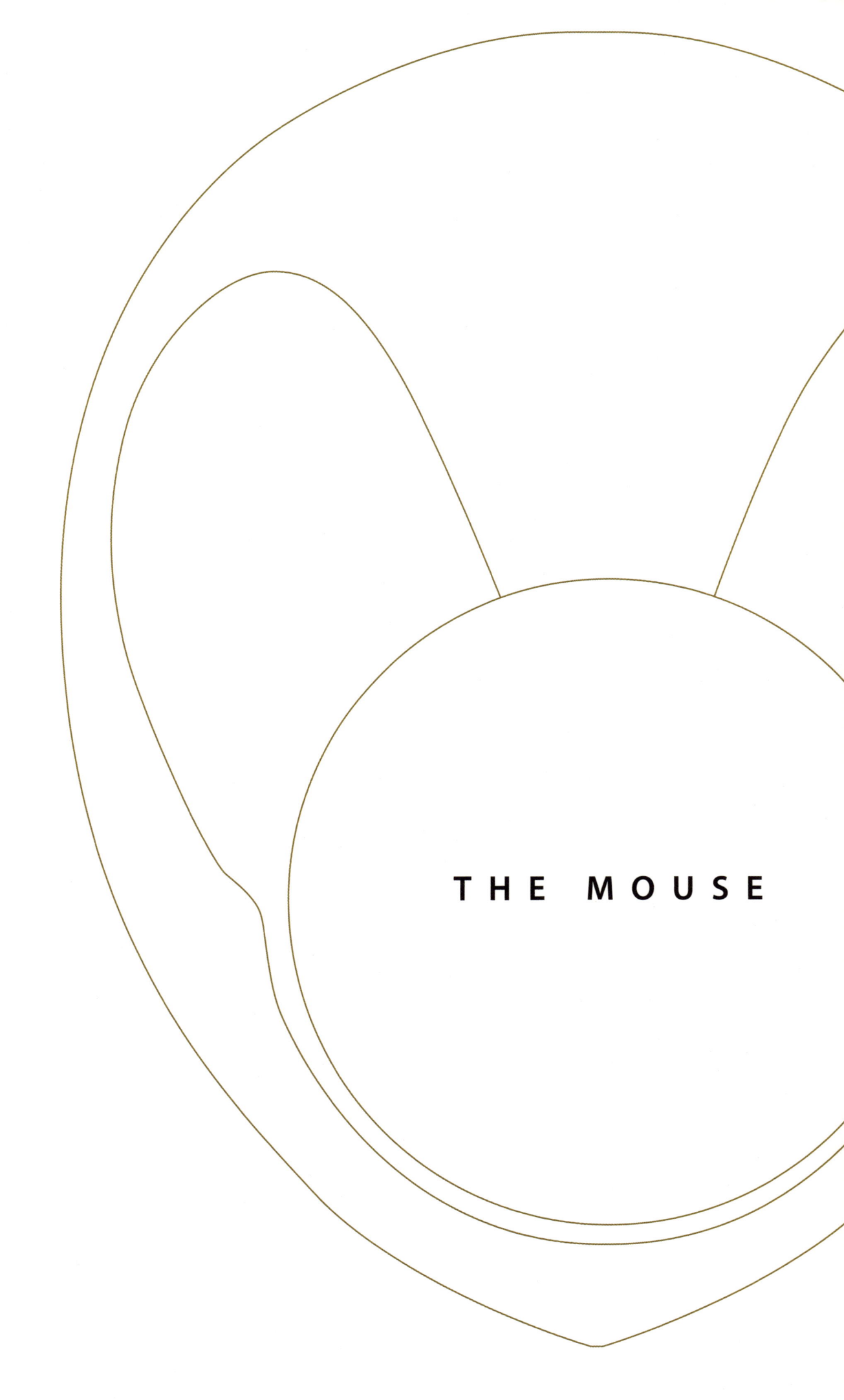

THE MOUSE

Initially going by the name of Mortimer, he became Micky Mouse and conquered the whole world from 1928.

The ancient idea that dolphins are friends of humans has been brought into question in more recent years. The animals' "smile", their love of playing and musical "sense" have kept the idea of the friendly dolphin alive, and without forgetting their esteemed intelligence, long compared to that of chimpanzees. Recently, people have also talked about the "darker" side of these mammals who don't follow ships through playful instinct but are actually looking for edible leftovers. In terms of intelligence, crows appear to beat dolphins hand down, the latter in some circumstances, seeming as resistant to change as us humans who love them so much.

In the European context, the dolphin's popularity is linked to the story of Arion. Originally from the island of Lesbos, the son of Poseidon and the nymph Oncaea, was a sort of Mediterranean Orpheus, to whom we owe the invention of the dithyramb and perhaps even tragedy. Having participated in a musical competition in Sicily and won first prize, Arion set sail for Corinth. During a stopover at Taranto, his shipmates decided to kill him and steal all of the riches he was transporting. Faced with the choice of killing himself or throwing himself overboard, Arion asked if he could sing one last time. Accompanied by the *kithara*, he sang praise to Apollo, who sent his dolphins to save him. Arion managed to survive on the back of a dolphin but once ashore, he failed to put him straight back into the water and the dolphin died. But Periander – tyrant of Corinth and Arion's friend – took revenge over the murdering mariners at the dolphin temple he had built in its honour. The dead animal was catasterized as the constellation Delphinus.

Designated as the "sacred fish" by the Greeks, the dolphin is not a fish at all, but a cetacean with hot red blood running through its veins.

In Renaissance times, decorative dolphins became very popular. Indeed, they could not only be found in innumerable Roman fountains, but also as ornamentation on furniture, or architectural elements. Even the greatest artists experimented with this theme: in 1575, Giacomo della Porta created the magnificent Dolphin Fountain in Rome, with the stylized cetacean as an infinite source of water. Bernini sculpted a *Putti on a dolphin* (1617), and we probably owe *Neptune with dolphin* to him too.

The most beautiful encounter between man and the mythical animal is a Roman marble statue from the beginning of our era by an anonymous sculptor. Indeed, in *Eros and the dolphin*, the god of love and the mythical animal are embraced in a spiralling gesture, as if the incantatory power of the waves were intent on sweeping Eros himself away.

THE DOLPHIN

In 1575, Giacomo della Porta achieved the magnificent Dolphin Fountain in Rome, with the stylized cetacean as an infinite source.

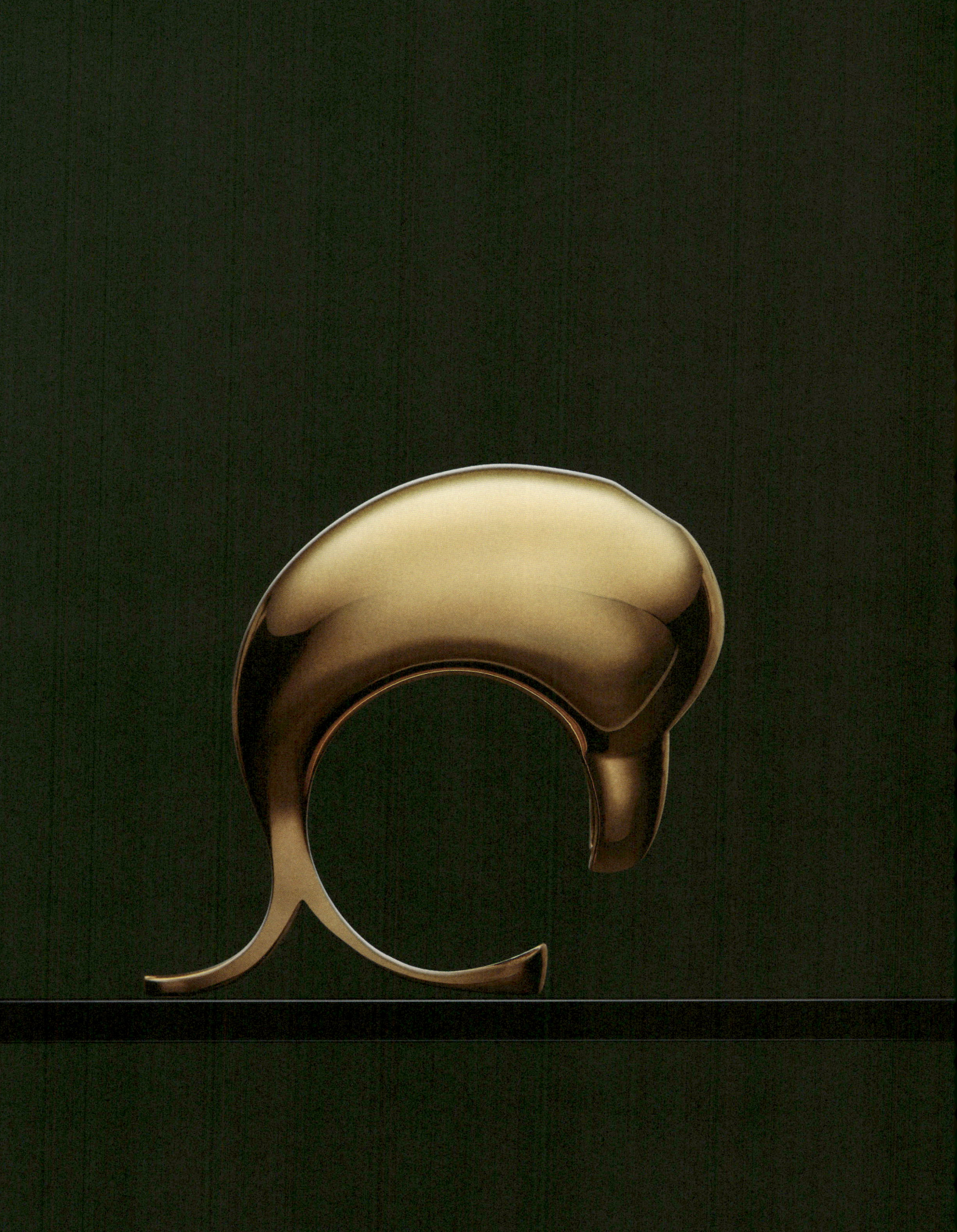

*F*or the ancient Egyptians, one of the most well-known snakes, the immense cosmic snake, Apopis, represents the forces of chaos which existed before the creation and who, exiled to the outskirts of the cosmos at this precise moment, perpetually threatened the work of the creator.

Looking at the snake on a mythical level we find a precious guide in the person of Aby Warburg, who focused on the tales of the Pueblo Indians during their ritual snake dance. The real basis for these myths is the extreme dryness of the habitat of these Colorado Indians, a situation which had to be addressed whatever the cost, by creating possibilities for the rain to return.

As the deity of meteorology, the snake was supposed to ensure lightening, heralding on a symbolic level the arrival of the redeeming waters. During this ceremony, the dancers were transformed into snakes by subjecting themselves to the force and power of an animal they believed to be a higher being. In this context, the dancer and the snake were completely at one, and this is clearly visible notably in the ritual dance of the inhabitants of Walpi, who carried living rattlesnakes and spun around with them. Carried out by masked initiates, the dance gave the privileged animals an active role.

The snake appeared, in other terms, as the central element and the "sun" in a system of thought that questioned the "whys and wherefores". The metamorphosis operated on a symbolic level by the Pueblo Indians allowed them to go beyond the negativity and danger linked to the figure of the snake by making it their partner. This solution radically differs from the biblical image of the snake which remained locked in its innate negativity, whether it's the diabolical animal undermining the perfect construction of the garden of Eden or in the Babylonian context, where it appeared as a symbol of seduction and decadence.

Greek culture developed the myth of the snake by presenting two radically different aspects. The first corresponds to Dionysian violence: it was in the form of snakes that Zeus and Rhea gave life to their monstruous daughter Persephone, and it was once again disguised as a snake that Zeus seduced his own daughter, resulting in the birth of Dionysos. This harmful lineage is also present in the legend of Laocoon: his terrible death, inflicted through vengeance of the gods and accomplished by two giant snakes, who gobble him up after killing his children, gives way to a man-snake configuration expressing the *summum* of human suffering as well as a tragic pessimism.

The other side of Greek tradition is occupied by Asclepius, the Greco-Roman god of medicine. His caduceus is a short baton with a snake wrapped around it. The secret knowledge of the underworld (and notably the use of plants that the snakes passed on to Asclepius), as well as the fact of changing skin and being reborn, make the snake the ideal symbol of healing and immortality.

THE SNAKE

*Animal undermining the perfect construction
of the Garden of Eden*

*E*ven the words we use to talk about butterflies immediately show their importance not just in the field of imagination, but also metaphysics and psychology. Depending on the different stages of their development, we refer to the egg, pupa, nymph, and imago. There are, however, many more. Much of the discourse around metamorphosis, and more specifically metempsychosis, refers to butterflies too.

But what exactly is a butterfly, since this "winged insect", as Aristotle already called it, exists in four steps or stages, as if matter was crystalised in the different forms of the egg, larva (with its sloughing), the chrysalis, stuck in its superb immobility, and finally, the butterfly itself? Although once it reaches completeness this animal no longer feeds and spends its time procreating, in turn producing eggs, with a lifespan of just a few weeks on average, it also appears to be truly immortal, belonging to a cyclic movement of nature that relentlessly renews itself. Hence the famous adage from the great Lao Tse: "What the caterpillar calls the end, the rest of the world calls a butterfly".

And so, due also to the fact that the Greek word *psyche* (originally: breath) means both butterfly and soul, butterflies are the preferred animal form of both philosophers and poets. For philosophers, the body is nothing more than a tomb, a prison; thanks to metempsychosis, the soul is purified through a series of births and reincarnations. It definitively leaves its prison, and it does this by flying away, just like a butterfly. With pre-Socratic philosophy, the psyche is designated as the vital force, the basis of a living being's movement, the same force we find in the different phases of the life of a butterfly.

In his dialogue *Phaedrus*, Plato speaks of the "winged chariot" and adds: "These wings lift up heavy things to where the gods dwell and are nourished and grow in the presence of the wisdom, goodness, and beauty of the divine".

In a key passage of book XV of *Metamorphoses*, Ovid attributes the following words to Pythagoras: "Do you not see that whatever bodies are consumed by length of time, or by dissolving heat, are changed into small animals? The warlike steed, buried in the ground, is the source of the hornet. […] The silkworms, too, that are wont to cover the leaves with their white threads, a thing observable by husbandmen, change their forms into that of the deadly moth". The whole world of nature is in the image of the butterfly.

THE BUTTERFLY

*What the caterpillar calls the end,
the rest of the world calls a butterfly.*

*I*n 1899, an American expedition discovered hundreds of crocodile mummies in Egypt, instead of the human ones they were expecting to find. The archaeologists looked more closely when they discovered papyrus inside the mummified animal remains, but this did not stop them from emptying them out and then throwing them away. The fact that crocodiles had been mummified shows perfectly how these creatures were once the object of ancient worship.

There were numerous myths across the African continent concerning these scaly beings and their cult remained firmly in embedded in people's minds. And so, in the Ivory Coast crocodiles appeared on sculpted doors or even on the scales used to weigh gold. Among the Dogon tribes in Mali, crocodiles are representatives of the *nommo*, the first primitive being created by the combined action of the earth, seas and sky. In Burkina Faso, the crocodile is both feared and admired; it is dangerous but, at the same time, its apotropaic version is beneficial.

Present for almost 3000 years in ancient Egyptian culture, the figure of Sobek, the man-falcon-crocodile god, was sometimes associated with Horus. The centre of Sobek cult was Fayoum, in Lower Egypt with its capital Crocodilopolis: some sacred animals were bred there, priests made offerings to the crocodiles, and this was where the specimens mentioned earlier were solemnly mummified. Some of these crocodiles sometimes carried their offspring on their backs, reflecting the specificity of these animals who take great care of their descendants. Sobek was also worshipped in another great sanctuary, Kom-Ombo, in Upper Egypt, which he shared with Horus the Elder. Today there is a museum dedicated to him near the temple.

A Namibian legend recounts how crocodile skin, often considered repugnant, came about. Originally, the crocodile had a magnificent golden skin which remained intact as it only hunted at night. During the day, the other animals came to admire its skin. Seeing how everyone adored him, the crocodile grew vain and started coming out of the water during the day too, and all the other animals turned their backs on him. Exposed to the African sun, its skin became thicker and ugly. The shame it felt ever since forced it to disappear under the water, until it became invisible.

The crocodile, also known as "crocodelle" in French, can live up to a hundred years old. It can be considered as a precious talisman or, in its mixed *talimbi* form, half-animal, half-human, represent the source of great danger.

THE CROCODILE

The center of Sobek cult was Fayoum in Lower Egypt whose capital was called Crocodilopolis.

We associate birds with flight and song. They appear to be delicate and sensitive creatures, except when we think of birds of prey. The *Metamorphoses*, which so delighted Antiquity, nevertheless tell a rather sordid tale, the one of Procne and Philomela, the two daughters of Pandion, King of Athens. As part of his stratagem, the King of Thrace, Tereus, Procne's husband, invites his beautiful sister-in-law Philomela. He rapes her in a hut, cuts out her tongue and leaves her for dead. Philomela survives and sends a message woven on a tapestry to her sister, who plots a dreadful revenge. Indeed, the two sisters kill Itys, the son of Procne and Tereus, cut him up, cook him and serve him to his father who eats him. Furious with rage after discovering the truth, he plots to kill the two women, transformed *in extremis* by the gods into a nightingale (Procne) and a swallow (Philomela). Tereus is transformed into a hoopoe and Itys a goldfinch.

For the Greeks, the movement of birds in the sky carried a meaningful message. Hence in the *Odyssey*, the third appearance of an eagle with a dove in its mouth heralds the massacre of the suitors on Ulysees' return.

As for the Romans, birdwatching was truly a state affair. Based on signs left in the sky by eagles, vultures, owls, ravens, or crows, they developed an "augury science", interpreted by a college of priests, the famous augurs.

It was with Leonardo da Vinci that interpreting bird behaviour left the speculative domain of divination when the artist started studying their movements. At a young age, he would already observe the elegant arabesques of the red kite in the Val d'Arno. Later, Leonardo dissected the birds' bodies and studied all aspects of flight, air density, winds, currents, resistance and even put forward aerodynamic explanations, anticipating research which is still not outdated some 500 years later. The Tuscan genius also designed flying "machines" based on bird flight. We do not know if he actually constructed mechanical birds whose origin dates back to Antiquity, but he did however build a mechanical lion, shown in Milan in 1499. Philo of Byzantium and Hero of Alexandria had designed birds that sung, powered by steam and air pressure.

In the seventeenth century, Salomon de Caus improved the workings of these mechanical birds by using his barrel organs. Particularly popular at a time when people were passionate about bird song, from 1750 on, canaries were rivalled by the serinette, a bird automaton which could play up to nine different tunes. Thus, the history of artificial birds crosses paths with that of mechanical birds, clockmaking, and gold and silver work. And so, a mighty but miniscule animal has been at the origins of a series of technical and cultural revolutions.

THE BIRD

*Philon of Byzantium and Ateron of Alexandria had designed birds
that sung, powered by steam and air pressure.*

The famous legend of the Inaba hare had already appeared as early as the eighth century, in the *Kojiki*, the first chronicle in Japan. Well-known in the period preceding the first Japanese emperor, the hare was said to have convinced some sharks or crocodiles to form a kind of bridge which he could then cross without difficulty. Realising they had been duped, the aquatic animals took their revenge by ripping off the hare's fur. When he and his brothers were looking for their sister, Yagami, the god Okuninushi, "master of the great country", came across the hare. Whilst the evil brothers advised the creature to bathe in the sea – which could have killed him – kind Okuninushi helped him to heal his wounds using pollen from a magical plant and consequently saved him.

This myth, which also exists in Indonesia, brings a small, delicate and weak terrestrial animal face to face with particularly strong and ferocious marine animals. The theme of regenerated skin is also associated with the moon and is even found outside of the Asian context. And so, according to the well-known legend, the hare, willing to sacrifice his own life to save the Chinese emperor from starvation (disguised as a poor pilgrim), was transformed into a jade hare living in the Moon Palace.

La Fontaine was well acquainted with hares in his role as Master of Waters and Forests near Château-Thierry, and they often appeared in his *Fables* from the 1660s. Even though it is the hunter who speaks first ("I send a shot/ at some unsuspecting rabbit"), the peaceful image is quickly recreated: "Again I see the rabbits more light-hearted than ever coming close under my death-dealing hand". It's as if these animals were capable of reproducing in an unlimited way, to satisfy not just the disinterested tenderness of the innocent gaze but also the interested perspective of the master hunter of nature.

A more complicated reality – above all in the human world – also appears in a short fable by Perrault: "The eagle chasing a rabbit was asked by a scarab beetle [a coleoptera] to let him live, but it didn't listen and gobbled up the rabbit. To get its revenge, for the next two years the scarab beetle broke the eagle's eggs who eventually laid its eggs on Jupiter's cloak. The beetle dropped his muck on the cloak. Wanting to shake it off, Jupiter threw the eggs down below and broke them". This story was illustrated in the 29th Fountain of the Versailles Labyrinth, whilst in other princely gardens, such as Boboli in Florence, real rabbits inhabited an island much to the delight of its visitors.

The most mysterious rabbit is of course the one in Lewis Carroll's novel. It is by following this strange animal with his pocket watch that Alice and the readers fall down a rabbit hole and then into a well in order to discover Wonderland, an unkwnown realm, nonetheless so similar to our own.

THE RABBIT

*The rabbit was transformed into a jade hare
who lived in the Moon Palace…*

November 18, 1487, the ambassador Mohamed Ibn-Mahfuz delivered a gift in Florence, from the Sultan of Egypt, Al-Achraf Sayf ad-Dîn Qa'it Bay, known as Qait Bay. Offered to Lorenzo the Magnificent, who was passionate about his menagerie, the precious gift was a live giraffe which caused much excitement in the town of the Medici. Artists, including the great Vasari, embodied it in their paintings, poets sang the praises of the strange animal, intellectuals were in awe at discovering its tiny horns. Lorenzo even promised to send this creature (the ultimate exotic animal) to Anne of France but was unable to keep his promise as the giraffe, far from home, died prematurely.

During Antiquity, Italy had already seen another rather solemn appearance of a giraffe. When he returned triumphant from Egypt in 46 BC, Julius Cesar had a giraffe in his list of trophies. Presented for the very first time in Europe, the animal was known as a *cameleopardalis*, or camel-leopard. In an act of supreme contempt – even such a rare beast did not mean anything to the master of the world –, Cesar sacrificed his giraffe by feeding it to the hungry lions in the amphitheatre of the temple of Venus Genetrix.

The appearance of this unique mammal made such an impact that it was mentioned by some of the greatest ancient authors, such as Varro, Diodorus of Sicily, Strabo, Pausanias, Heliodorus, and many others. All emphasise its docility (Pliny the Elder called it *ovis ferae*, a wild ewe) and Heliodorus even affirmed that it could be taken for a walk quite peacefully with a short rope around its neck.

In any case, the giraffe is a superlative being. This tallest of all terrestrial animals – a mammal with hooves – is also the biggest known herbivorous ruminant. Its long neck is the result of extreme adaptation because it allows the animal to survive in the wooded steppe, reaching the level of vegetation essential to its survival. Giraffes live in small groups, sometimes alongside zebras, another exceptional animal with an appearance that is not easily forgotten.

The giraffe constellation, situated in the Northern hemisphere, between the Great Bear and Cassiopeia, was discovered and given its name by Jacob Bartsch, assistant and son-in-law of the great Kepler. Bartsch invented a whole celestial bestiary, creating the Cockerel, Columba, the Unicorn, the Fly, and the White Tiger. Today giraffes are an endangered species. Exposed to climate change, they are losing their natural habitat and, above all, their main food source, acacias. If nothing changes soon, all that will remain is the constellation.

THE GIRAFFE

Intellectuals were in awe at discovering its tiny horns...

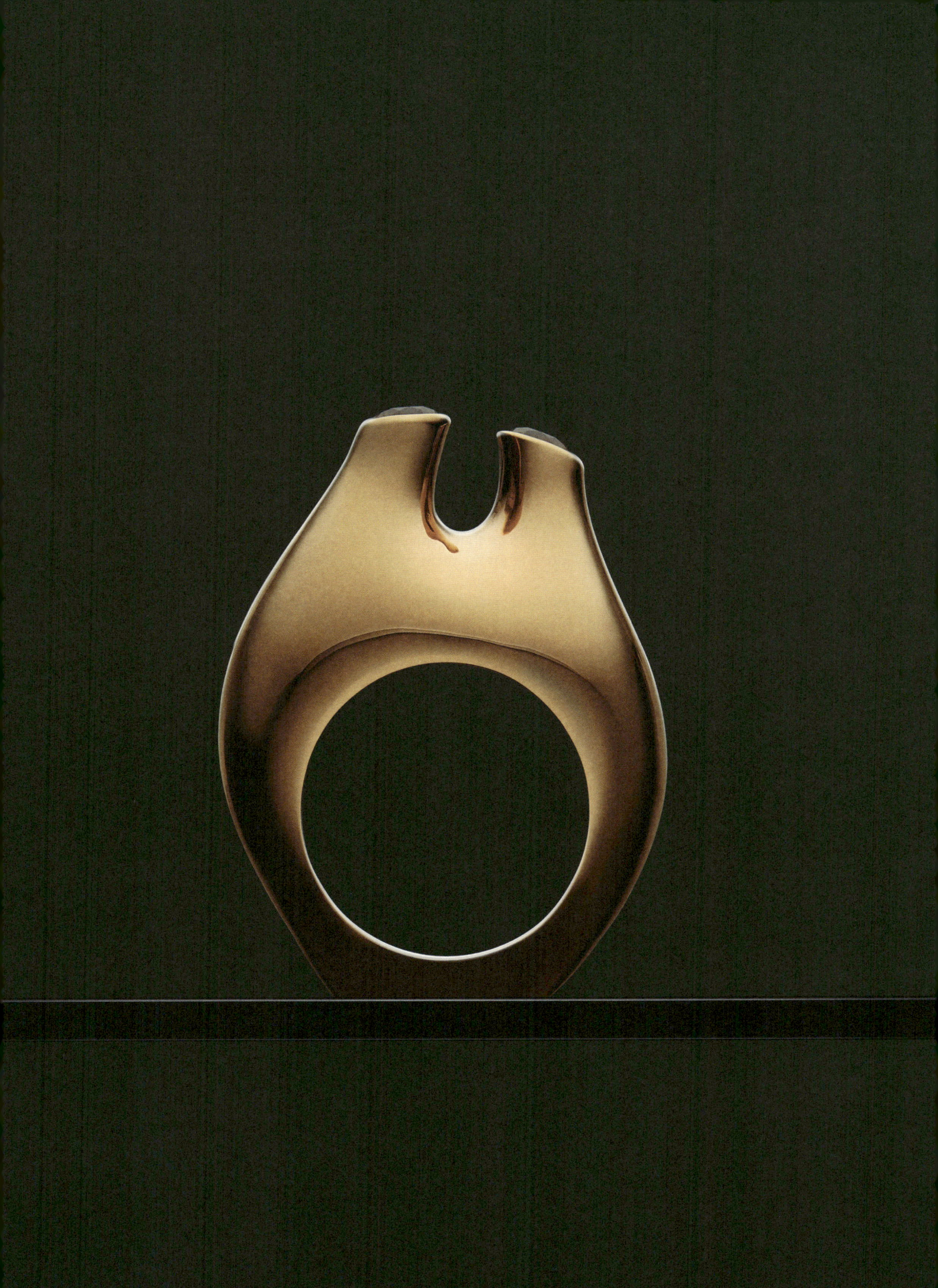

*T*he kind of modern prose that has shaped our vision of the world speeds ahead like a horse in mid galop. Horses were a great favourite in the work of two of its key protagonists, Montaigne and Cervantes, who used them in a rather specific manner. In their texts, the climactic moment is announced by the falling off a horse.

Around 1573, Montaigne, was overtaken by someone riding "full galop" and fell from his "little horse". He lost consciousness and was plunged into a state of "inexpressible sweetness". After affirming he would rather "die on horseback than in his bed", in the *On training* chapter, Montaigne explains how he discovered his inner "self" during this accident, namely the object that was to become the focus of his famous *Essays*.

In a key scene from Cervantes' novel, Don Quixote "charged at Rocinante's fullest gallop and fell upon the first mill that stood in front of him; but as he drove his lance-point into the sail the wind whirled it round with such force that it shivered the lance to pieces, sweeping with it horse and rider, who went rolling over on the plain, in a sorry condition."

We find, this overly-exaggerated interest for falling off horses in Stendhal's work who affirmed having "spent his life falling off horses". Yet, in the 19th-century writer's work, this humiliating incident of falling off a horse is at the same time an initiatory one, or better still, transformed into an erotic triumph. Indeed, there is nothing more seductive than recounting one's own fall "in front of the ladies". The romantic poet Clemens Brentano understood this perfectly stating: "Passions are horses". And what of Nietzsche who, in January 1889, was devastated when he saw a horse violently whipped by his coachman – heralding his own, forthcoming intellectual "fall"?

All these episodes reflect the negative side of a fantasy world which, in its victorious version, sanctifies the horse and transforms it into a magical, mythical animal, horse-friend or other. In Europe, this cult was at its height during the Middle Ages. According to Paul Virilio, the viewpoint of those who looked down on the world from above changed human history, because the man-horse partnership allowed complete visual control whilst at the same time ensuring the knight could carry out his actions at astounding speed.

Even though the magic of chivalry had disappeared by Cervantes' time, it managed to survive in the field of art. Horses from the art group The Blue Rider, from Transavanguardia, or the very real ones, presented by Jannis Kounellis, remind us of our somewhat ambivalent love of these most exceptional animals.

THE HORSE

Montaigne affirmed he would rather die on horseback than in his bed…

*A*bove all, we know Aries thanks to the constellation of the same name, heralding springtime. It's a cardinal sign, associated with fire and the planet Mars: hence John Foxton's *Cosmografia*, from 1408, shows a small ram on top of the Greek god of war's head.

In Greece, it was known as *Chrysomallos*, a talking, flying ram with a golden fleece. Before taking its place in the sky, the ram laid its fur – the mythical golden fleece – on an oak tree, in a lair guarded by a snake who never slept.

In Egypt, the god Banebdjedet, Lord of Mendes and main deity of this town in Lower Egypt, was worshipped as the god of fecundity. His sacred animal was initially *Ovis longipes palaeoaegyptiaca* with its horizontal spiralling horns, then, after it became extinct, a ram with curved horns called *Ovis Platyra aegyptiaca*.

As for the Ancient Egyptians, they associated the signs of the Zodiac with precious stones. Amethyst, for example, was linked to Aries, topaz to Cancer, beryl to Leo, cornelian to Libra, emerald to Sagittarius and sapphire to Aquarius.

In French, rams were long known as "belins", or uncastrated males of the *Ovis aries* species, from the Bovidae family. Appreciated for their intelligence, timidity, and excellent memory, they can also become very aggressive.

The symbolic form of the ram appears in many cultures across the world and is synonymous with young, healthy, strong males, bold and full of enthusiasm. This is how the ram is depicted in Caravaggio's rather surprising interpretation of *Saint John the Baptist*, from 1602. The pagan joy of life of the naked young man with the mischievous smile, strong and handsome (most likely Cecco, the artist's model and lover), perfectly expresses the ram's legendary qualities. By substituting the lamb – *Agnus Dei* –, the usual symbol of Saint John the Baptist, with the ram, Caravaggio erotises the scene: the animal with the spiral horns seems to be virtually kissing the young man. This tour de force opposed the religious character of the equally famous *Agnus Dei* by Zurbaran, made around 1635, a composition the Spanish artist reworked some six times, anticipating Warhol's serial representations.

Besides the magnificent golden fleece, the ram's most expressive element are its splendid horns. Their spiral form has given way to numerous interpretations, the favourite being the image of an initiatory pathway.

Charles Darwin was more prosaic and correct in being the first to believe that the structure of these horns had evolved due to their function in combats between rival males. Rams capable of beating other males could have more offspring and would pass on the gene for larger horns to their descendants. Moreover, different types of horns are used for different types of combat: short horns are used like bladed weapons, long horns are strictly intended for wrestling, whilst spiral horns are ideal for ramming.

THE RAM

*Synonymous with young, healthy strong males,
bold and full of enthusiasm…*

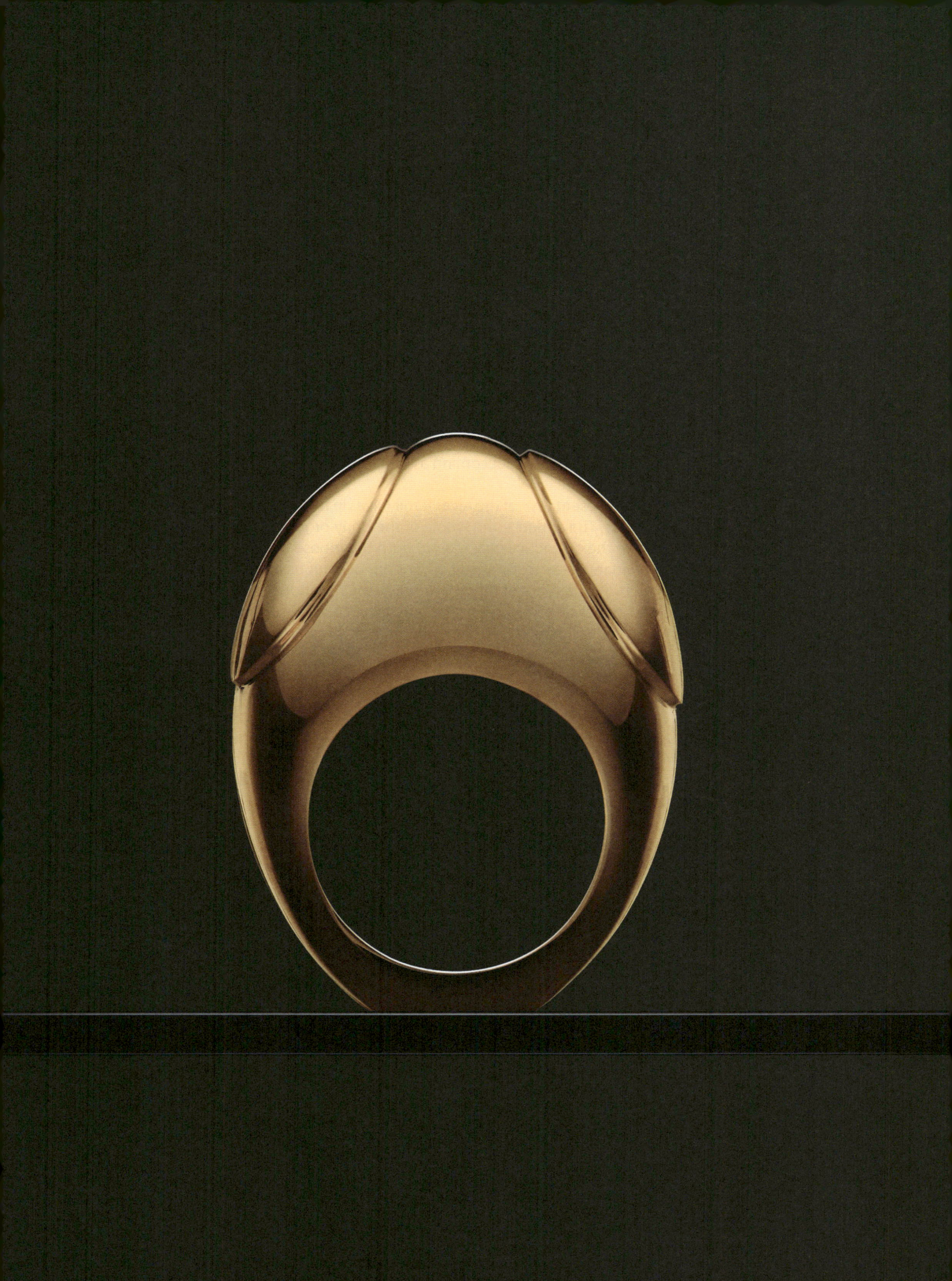

When we think of the world of shamans, we immediately imagine one animal: the elk. For the Yakuts in Siberia, the elk is the most masculine, most virile animal. Representing the reproductive male, it's associated with shamanic rites. The elk is the ultimate wild forest animal. Solitary by nature, the male keeps his distance from the other animals, except during the breeding season from September to October. Its imposing antlers are the exterior sign of its power (only males have them), and this already attracted the attention of artists at the time of prehistoric cave painting.

In the past, these animals were very common in Europe, whilst today they are only found in Scandinavian countries or zoos. Elks are becoming as rare as shamans.

The moose, the other representative of the Alces family, lives in the United States and Canada; its biggest enemy are ticks. The antlers – the whole of the bony organs on its head which can grow extremely big – are the distinctive character of both the moose and the male elk. Unlike the horns of other Cervidae, these vascularised organs are deciduous; they fall off every year in late winter, replaced by new antlers. In the spring, when the new bone structure develops, it is surrounded by tissue, or velvet, to protect it. The antlers reach their maximum development at breeding season; the animals often try to get rid of them at this point by rubbing up against trees.

Antlers have several functions: females are attracted to them and so they act as a secondary sexual signal; they protect the animal's head during combats, they are a visual reflection of the animal's rank and, according to some researchers, they also amplify sound like a parabolic reflector. The German painter Albrecht Dürer was fascinated by antlers; he added them to a mermaid's body and fused them onto the body of a dragon, the whole composition designed as a kind of grotesque chandelier.

Populations who speak Ob-Ugric languages, and notably the Khanty (Ostyaks), tell how the elk originally had six legs which made it so fast that no hunter could catch it; the Great Hunter and son of the mother earth hunted it relentlessly, but to no avail. One day, he found the elk near a lake and cut off two of his legs. The elk was then taken up to the skies to allow hunters to find their way.

Black Elk was the name of an important character in the tragic history of North American Indians. This chief of the Sioux and sacred man, whose real name was Hehaka Sapa, took part in the great battles of his time, including the one at Wounded Knee; he was part of Buffalo Bill's famous troop, converted to Catholicism and only returned to his ancestral religion towards the end of his life.

Its imposing antlers are the exterior sign of its power…

*I*n 802, a white elephant named Abul Abbas arrived in Aix-la-Chapelle after a very long voyage. The animal, given to Charlemagne by the famous Haroun-al-Rachid and accompanied by Isaac, the emperor's diplomate, had left India for Bagdad. It then embarked at Carthage for Liguria, crossed the Alps a thousand years after Hannibal, and finally arrived at the emperor's court. Exposed in an ostentatious manner at different sites across the Empire, this sign of royalty mentioned in chronicles of the time survived in popular memory. The event is related to the proverbial white elephants of South-East Asia. Symbolising on the one hand monarchic power, peace and prosperity, light-skinned elephants were, on the other hand, unusable and expensive to keep, because they weren't allowed to work and needed food and looking after. The famous Phileas Barnum had bought for his circus a white elephant called Toung Taloung from the King of Siam, an animal who turned out to be more grey than white, hence the ironic designation a "white elephant" to talk about something enormous without any immediate utility.

The elephant, characterised by Buffon as "a miracle of intelligence and a monster of matter" was the object of exaggerated anthropomorphisation, and attached to the observance of various cults, the adoration of the Sun and the Moon, ablutions before adoration, divination, piety towards the Heavens… The eighteenth century was fascinated by the mystery surrounding elephantine mating habits. Hence, the author of *Natural History* drew a picturesque image of the animal's breeding rituals: "When the females are on heat, […] they separate into couples created beforehand through desire; they choose each other freely, they hide […]. We never saw them mating, above all they fear being seen by their kinsmen and know perhaps better than us the pure pleasure of climaxing in silence and of focusing uniquely on their beloved partner".

The idea that elephants never reproduce in captivity, associated with their modesty (already mentioned in Aristotle and Plini the Elder), has led us to forget the amorous fury of the male elephant in favour of the virtuous, idealised pachyderm. It should also be said that Buffon never actually managed to observe the object of his study directly, since the first elephant exhibited in France was the one presented at the Saint-Germain fair in Rue Dauphine, in 1771.

The elephant's most significant feature is its trunk. This long pipe, also called proboscis, is truly a multi-functional organ. The trunk, made up of muscles and nerves, contains numerous blood vessels. It is the result of a fusion between the nose and upper lips and is used for gripping food, as a suction pump, a snorkel, but also quite simply to drink, touch, or smell.

THE ELEPHANT

A miracle of intelligence and a monster of matter…

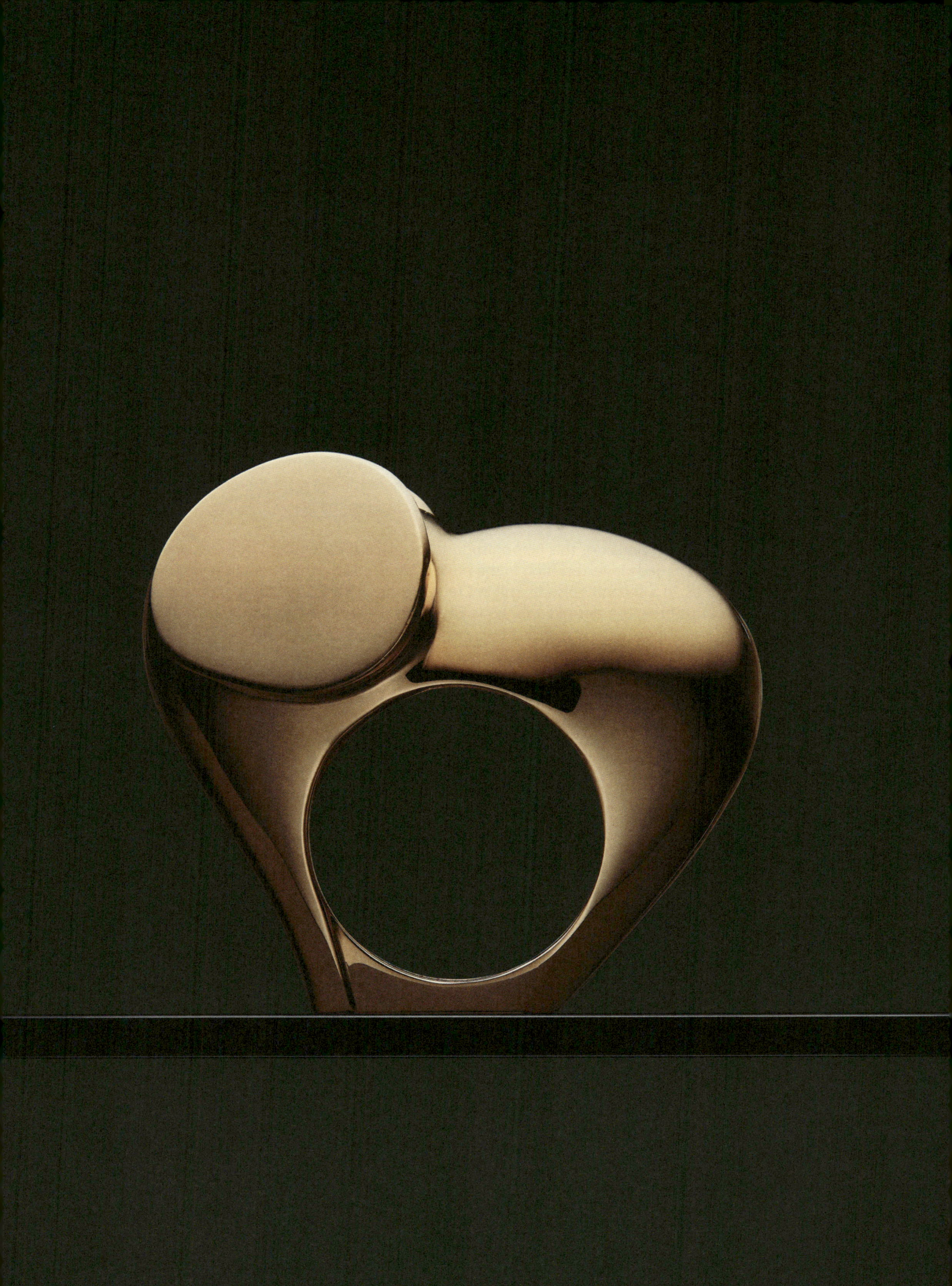

*T*o understand the bull, what better than to ask who were the mythical women besotted with him and how did their romantic encounter actually take place. The first of these feminine figures is of course Europa, the daughter of the Phoenician King Agenor. In a toned down, Gilbert & George style version, Roberto Calasso imagined their famous relationship thus: "But how did all that begin? […] Europa and her friends were picking daffodils, hyacinths, violets, roses, and some thyme. […] Suddenly, they found themselves surrounded by a herd of bulls. Among them, there was a dazzling white one, with small horns that looked like sparkling precious stones. His expression belied the threat. To such an extent that Europa, initially timid, drew her flowers close to the bull's snowy white muzzle. Like a little dog, the bull moaned with pleasure, threw himself on the grass, and allowed Europa to place the garland on his little horns. The princess dared to mount him amazon-style. Then without warning, the herd moved from the dried up riverbed towards the beach and with false uncertainty, moved closer to the water".

As we know, the climax of this first episode takes place on the island of Crete, where our founding couple made love, resulting in the birth of three children, including the famous King of Crete, Minos. In a second episode, still in Crete, we move from light, diurnal passion to the monstrous. This time, the desired woman is Pasiphaë, queen and wife of Minos. In the best-known version, Minos had to sacrifice a bull every year in honour of Poseidon.

Once possessing a particularly beautiful bull in his herd, the King of Crete believed he had duped the god by replacing it with the animal that was to be sacrificed. In revenge, Poseidon forced Pasiphaë to lust after a white bull. To fulfil her desire (given that she could not change her form like Zeus), she asked Dedalus to build her a large wooden heifer, covered in real cow hide, which fooled the white bull and allowed their unnatural union. The fruit of this act was the third appearance of a bull in the form of the Minotaur.

These stories, woven around the figure of the bull, are quite remarkable if we read them as a mythical anthropology of love and, above all, love exposed to violence. Indeed, the first and second stories of the white bull are similar. The original scene of the encounter between Zeus (disguised as a bull) and Europa is, undoubtedly, extremely tender, but it is also a rape. The coupling between Pasiphaë, the "wide-shining", and the bull, vehicle of divine revenge, is the perverse expression of mad, uncontrolled desire, but it also reflects a fascination with the ecstatic encounter with a superpowered other, symbolized so well by the bull.

In other terms, these bull-related relationships take us back to the origins of sexuality – that is the origin of all of us –, a more troubling and more unusual version than the one we think of normally.

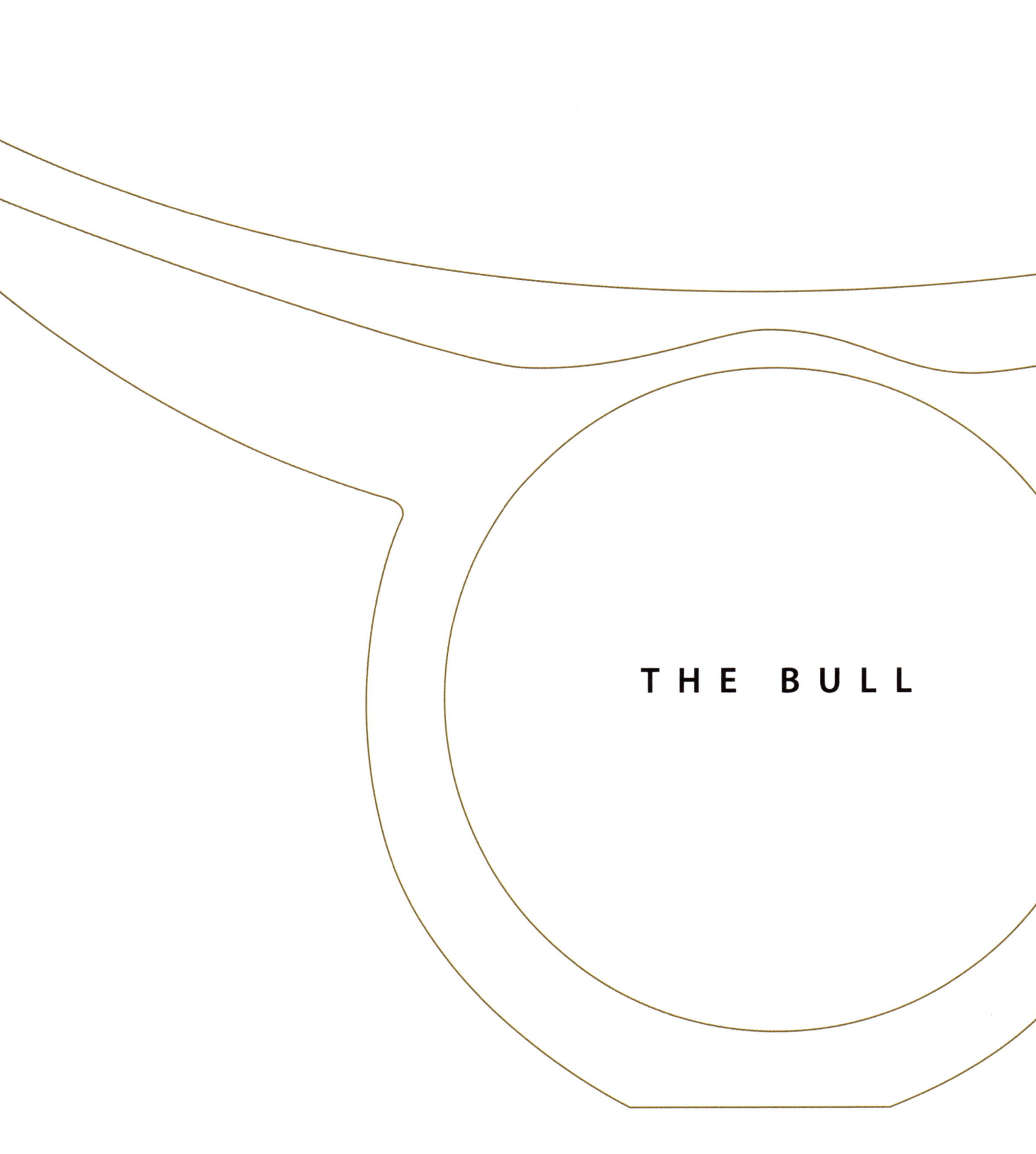

THE BULL

*The first of his female conquests is of course Europa,
the daughter of the Phoenician King Agenor…*

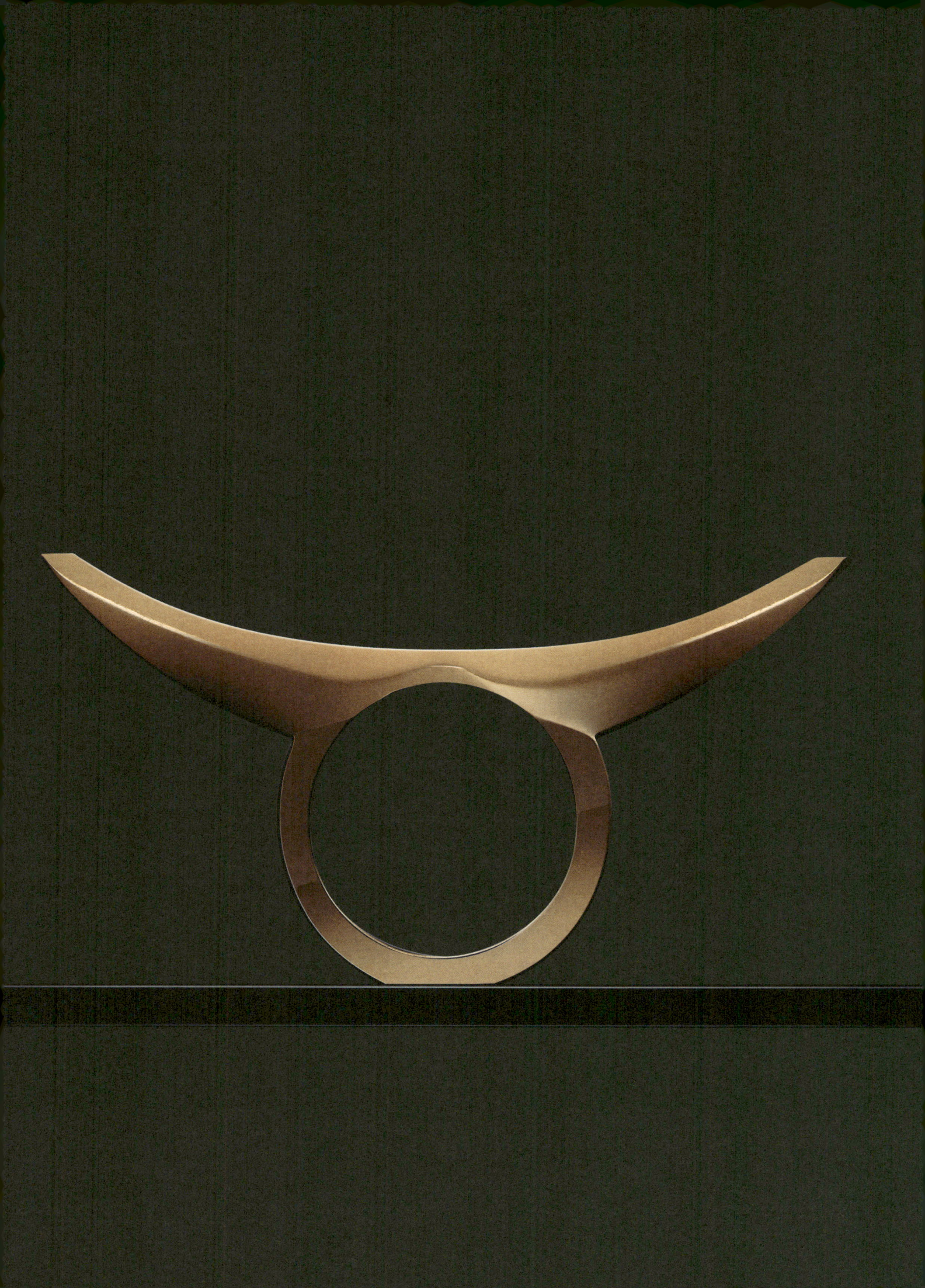

Almost all owls are rather solitary nocturnal birds of prey. They fall into two distinct categories; true or typical owls belong to the Strigidae family, while barn-owls (*Tyto alba*) are part of the Tytonidae. In most languages, owls have poetic names. In English there are some twenty species of screech owls, including the crested owl, the maned owl, the elf owl, the scops owl, the flammulated owl, the long-whiskered owlet, or the collared owlet. Other owls are named after their original habitat, such as the Puerto Rican owl, the Cuban screech-owl, the Jamaican owl, the Papuan hawk-owl.

In Egyptian hieroglyphics, the owls symbolized death, night, and passivity, and heralded the sun setting into the sea, giving way to darkness. In Aztec mythology, the owl embodied Techolotl, the god of the underworld. In Mayan culture, the horned owl is found in some sacred doomsday writings, while in Yucatan the common owl was nicknamed "the bird of lament" and associated with death. An Indian fable dating from around the third century AD, the Panchatantra, compares the god of death, Yama, to the owl; in the epic tale of the Mahabharata, the owl, symbol of darkness and night, is the opposite of the vulture, linked to the sun and daytime. Traces of this mythological opposition can also be found in other civilizations.

But we are certainly not out of the woods yet with these huge-eyed nocturnal birds who have always haunted our human dreams. So, let's be guided by the zoological data covering around 200 species, all with eyes too big for their heads but which nevertheless have one key particularity: their eyes are fixed like a camera lens and it's the bird's head that moves, offering almost a 270° vision.

Undoubtedly because of its huge eyes, which never miss a trick, the owl of Athena was a very important mythological bird, linked to the virgin goddess of knowledge, wisdom and erudition. This is why it often appeared on emblems for libraries, bookshops, universities, or learned societies. The Romans worshipped its prophetic capacities: hence an owl flying by could herald a defeat, or even death. Laying one of the bird's feathers near someone sleeping was said to make them talk and reveal their secrets. Still in Rome, these birds were sometimes nailed alive to the doors of houses, a custom that survived into the Middle Ages when their sacrifice was supposed to protect from lightning strikes and hailstones.

Like virtually all animals, owls were both feared and admired. By distinguishing itself from the nocturnal bird synonymous with danger, the origin of the peace-loving version probably lies in its resemblance to a human face. An owl flying at dusk is one of the most iconic images: the symbolic bird signifying the attainment of supreme knowledge.

THE OWL

*With these huge-eyed nocturnal birds who have
always haunted our human dreams…*

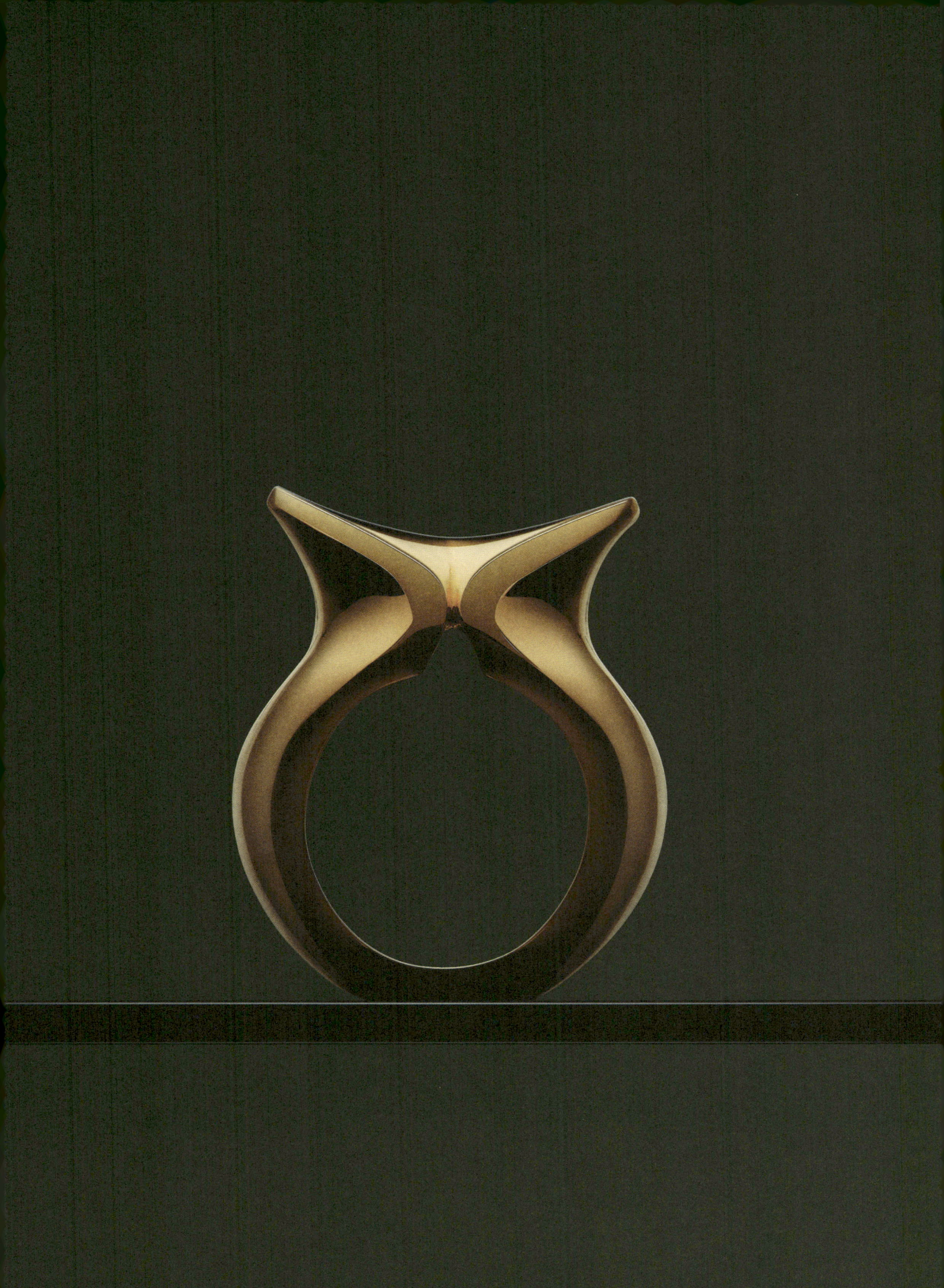

*I*n a mysterious painting from the Italian Renaissance by the artist Piero di Cosimo, *Venus, Mars and Cupid*, a series of animals surround the couple exhausted by their romantic encounter. There's a rabbit, symbol of fertility and lust, two doves, the expression of carnal love, and also – a detail that is perhaps hard to see – a butterfly delicately placed on the right leg of the goddess of love and beauty.

But where has it come from, in fact, this little insect, which is not strictly speaking a butterfly, but a moth, and more precisely a Jersey Tiger (*Euplagia quadripunctaria*) from the Erebidae family? Given that even well after the Renaissance the distinction between lepidoptera and moths remained very vague, it's the symbolic sense which appears more interesting in this case. Butterflies and love: this inevitable constellation reminds us of a story that once fascinated Antiquity, at least since Apuleius had given it its classical form in his *Golden Ass*.

The heroes are, in fact, the god of love Cupid and the soul-butterfly Psyche. Psyche, a girl as beautiful as Venus, makes the goddess jealous who then commissions her son Cupid to ensure Psyche meets only the ugliest of men. By shooting one of his famous arrows into his own leg and falling in love with Psyche, Cupid unites with the beauty, but they can only meet in darkness. Venus, frustrated once again, subjects Psyche to four tests which she miraculously overcomes, helped in part by some ants and an eagle. During the grand finale which sees the whole of Olympus reunited, Psyche, accepted at last, is given the wings of a butterfly, an apotheosis beautifully illustrated in *Love and Psyche* by Canova.

The delightful little detail added by Piero di Cosimo in the foreground of his composition, the one of love triumphing over war, or the butterfly placed on the body of the goddess, complicates everything. It reminds us that just when Venus seems fulfilled, the fact remains she is also jealous, she desires, doubts, in short, her life as a soul-butterfly is equally inscribed into the great universal war of love.

In his *Canzoniere*, Petrarch drew on the image of the "semplicetta farfalla", attracted by the shining light of his beloved, with the poetic I as the unfortunate embodiment of the moth overly exposed to the light.

For other authors, butterflies have been the source of a much more prosaic form of entomology: hence Vladimir Nabokov was passionate about hunting for rare butterflies, thus freeing the domain of love from the weight of metaphors and traditional animal comparisons.

THE NIGHT BUTTERFLY

But where has it come from, in fact, this little insect, which is not strictly speaking a butterfly, but precisely a Jersey Tiger…

When we are captured in its arms or tentacles, we are so frightened that we don't know where we are anymore. In fact, which is the top or the bottom? Where is the left or the right, when we are lost and engulfed by an octopus? "Gifted with exceptional capacities for camouflage and intimidation, one minute an alga, then a sponge, a rock or scarecrow", according to Roger Caillois, the octopus has "a vast repertoire of moves. It can easily fold its tentacles under its belly or curl them up over its head".

This astonishing energy and extreme versatility were already discussed in the famous passage from Pliny the Elder's *Natural History*. Here, we learn how the octopus managed to get out of the sea somewhere near Gibraltar, climb over fences and up trees looking for food, and even managed to open mussels with stones…

By definition octopuses are huge but, when they become disproportionate, they take on the Nordic form of the Kraken, the giant octopus inspired by the biblical Leviathan who attacks ships and forces them to capsize. It is so strange that Hawaiians consider them to be a species from a universe that preceded our own. Its immense eyes don't miss a trick and serve its equally extraordinary intelligence. Because octopuses think, and they do this not just by using their main brain, but also thanks to mini brains that work in conjunction with their tentacles. Just like its mimicry, the octopus has a proverbial capacity to change colour.

But legends around food also reflect irrational fear when faced with an octopus: although in the Mediterranean region people have always eaten octopuses, it is considered to be hard to digest and cause troubling dreams. The famous Diogenes of Sinope supposedly died following an indigestion caused by an octopus. As for the Church Fathers, they had no sympathy for our viscous creature, who knew how to wriggle its way in anywhere: for Saint Augustin, the octopus represented lies, treason and temptation, whilst Saint Basil saw it as the image of adulation, which reminds us however of its astonishing powers of seduction.

By looking straight into the eye of an octopus and perceiving something both intelligent and monstruous, man can see himself. It's therefore not surprising to see it transformed into the powerful symbol we can find on many Greek vases, Roman coins, or an uncountable number of mosaics. Thus, after having described it as "a true blaspheme of creation against itself", Victor Hugo can affirm in conclusion: "God made the octopus".

THE OCTOPUS

*A vast repertory of moves, it can easily fold its tentacles under its belly,
or curl them up over its head…*

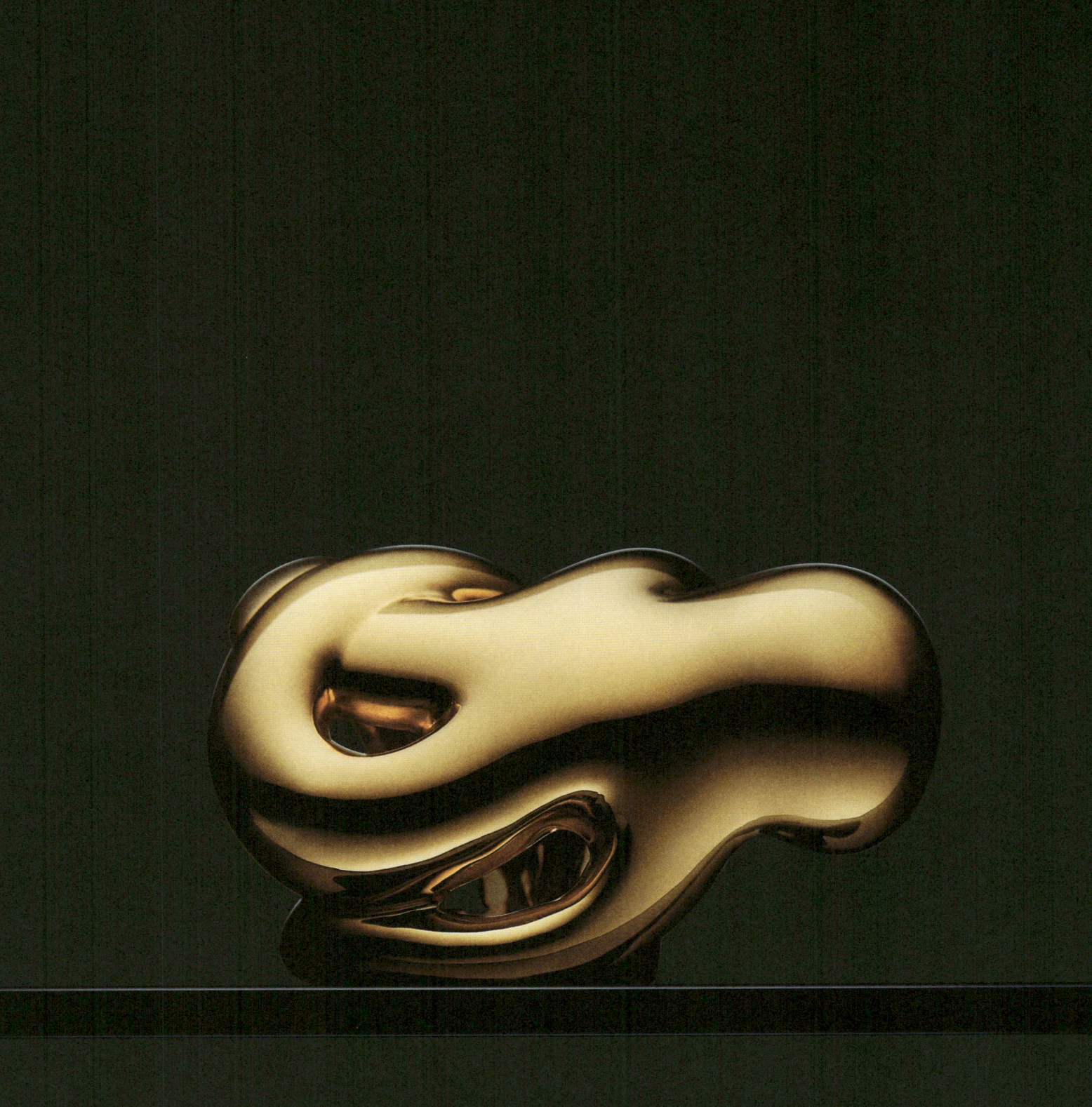

How would you capture the light of
the Mediterranean?
How would you reflect the formal beauty
of an Italian, French or English garden
in a piece of jewellery?
How would you frame nature in
a microcosm to display it at its best?
All these questions have fascinated Walid Akkad from
his childhood on the shores of the Mediterranean,
culminating in formal training at the French Jewellers
Guild, where he mastered the skills of casting,
polishing and setting stones.
Commissions and collaborations followed from
the great jewellery houses of Place Vendôme, then
Walid has been showcased at numerous international
exhibitions, in Paris, London, Geneva, Monaco,
New-York…
What makes his work so attractive? Is it that
he is involved in every step of the creative process
from initial, perfect architectural drawings to
exquisite prototypes, and then the fabulous
finished work, each one a sculptural masterpiece?
But look deeper and you will find behind this lie
three governing forces. The structural integrity
of the piece must be flawless. Next seek out just
the right stone – somehow it captures and then
reprojects the light with absolute mastery.
And lastly, will it enchant? Will it elicit a visceral,
sensual response – like the most intimate
whispered conversation?

Galerie Le "1"
1, rue de Lille 75007 Paris
contact@walidakkad.com
www.walidakkad.com

This book would never have been achieved without the friendly encouragements of Eric Coatalem, Christophe Donner, Caroline Van Hock, Jean-Philippe Hugo, Rabih Kayrouz, Karine Letayf, Isabelle & David Levy, Sylvie Lhermite-King, Diane & Sven Lingjaerde, Barbara Mariani, Frédérique Mattei, Garance Primant, Irina Rasquinet, Yasmina Sabrier & Monique Younes.
A special mention to Habib Charaf, Michael Jakob, Jean-Louis Mennesson, Michele Pizzi, Delphine Viala & Jérémy Zenou for their valuable help.
With my most heartfelt thanks to all.

Walid Akkad